eBook Publication for Training

eBook Publication
for Training

by Joel S. Zarley

COLUMBUS, OHIO MMXXI

eBook Publication for Training

Copyright © 2011 Purple Palm Media

ISBN-13: 978-0-9826523-2-9
ISBN-10: 0-9826523-2-1

www.purplepalmmedia.com
Email: editor@purplepalmmedia.com

Printed in the United States of America

Contents

Introduction

Why this Book?
The More Things Change…   3
The Past and Future of eBooks   3
About this Book   5
    Who is the Audience for this Book?   6

Chapter 1

What is an eBook?
The Trainer as Author & Publisher   9
What is an eBook?   9
The Advantages of eBooks in Learning   9
    Mobility   10
    Ease of Updating Content   10
    Cost Effective Publication   10
    Multimedia Capability*   10
    eReader "Plusses"   11
Disadvantages of eBooks?   12
    Lack of Comfort with Digital Reading   12
    Limited Distribution of eReaders   13
    Variations in Hardware & Software   13

Chapter 2

The Hardware: eReaders
The Age of the eReader   17
Displays: E Ink vs. LCD   17
Connectivity: How do Readers "Talk"?   18
Formats: What do they Read?   19
The eReader Platforms   19
    The Sony Reader   19
    The Amazon Kindle   20
    The Barnes & Noble Nook   20
    The Kobo eReader   20
    The Tablets   21
    Smartphones   21

Chapter 3

The Software: eBook Formats

eReaders Require Content   25
The Text Document Formats   25
Mark-Up Language Formats   26
Portable Document Format   26
eBook Formats   27
    Mobipocket   27
    EPUB   28

Chapter 4

Anatomy of an EPUB

Overview of the EPUB Format   31
    EPUB Features   31
Mechanics of the EPUB   32
    EPUB Specifications   32
    EPUB File Contents   33

Chapter 5

Producing an eBook: Workflow

Workflow at a Glance   37
Workflow Overview   37
    Write Content   37
    Format Content   37
    Publish   37
    Distribute   38

Chapter 6

Creating the Content

Creating Content: The Basics   41
    New or Existing Content?   41
Working with Various Tools   41
    Word Processors   42
    Page Layout Applications   42
    Web Page Development Tools   42
    Performance Support Development Tools   43

Chapter 7

Formatting the eBook

Why Format? I Like the Way it Looks! 47
Smashwords Style Guide 47
Tools for Formatting 48
Document Formatting Guidelines 48
    Save Your Work Under a New File Name 49
    Turn on the Show/Hide Feature 49
    Turn Off AutoCorrect & AutoFormat 49
    Eliminate Text Boxes 49
    Remove Styles & Normalize Text 50
    Remove Page & Section Breaks 50
    Images 50
    Other Items to Consider 50
Saving the Formatted File 51

Chapter 8

Publishing the eBook

Overview of the Publication Process 55
Creating the eBook Cover 55
Converting to EPUB 55
    Conversion within the Authoring Tool 56
    Conversion using Calibre 59
Layout & Format the Book 65
    Download & Install Sigil 65
    Opening & Working with EPUB Files 66
    Editing the eBook Content 68
    Styles & Stylesheets 70
    Working with eBook Mechanics 73
Testing the Finished Work 77
    EPUB Validation Check 77
    Test the Book in an eReader 78

Chapter 9

Distributing the eBook

Means of Distribution 81
eBook Management Software 81
    Calibre 81
    Adobe Digital Editions 82
    Apple iTunes 83
Manual File Management 83
    Wired Connection 84
    E-Mail 84
Retail Publication 84
    Amazon Kindle Store 84
    Barnes & Noble Nook Store 85
    Smashwords 85

Chapter 10

The Last Word

INTRODUCTION

Why this Book?

Why should a learning professional know about eBook technology? As an instructional designer, you have a lot more in common with authors and publishers than you may realize.

The More Things Change…

I became a trainer (and later, an instructional designer) in a corporate environment in 1989. It was with a small start-up telecommunications company that was a subsidiary of a larger hotel chain. (This was back in the early days of long distance deregulation when nearly everyone was launching their own telephone company.)

My initial responsibility in this role was to train new long distance operators in a two week classroom program. Like most new trainers, I grew into the role organically. I started as a call center operator; was promoted to shift supervisor; then finally became the call center's "trainer." Like a lot of people in this situation, I more "fell into" training than it being any sort of career plan. However, either by luck or by fate, I had found my professional calling.

In the early days of my training career, the technology available for developing learning materials was somewhat limited. I can recall doing "screen prints" of our call center software; photocopying them onto transparency sheets; then coloring them in with markers to emulate the color user screens. Then, I would use the resulting transparency mock-up of our screens on an overhead projector to teach new operators how to use the software. (Not only was this long before the days of "screen cam" software, it was also before most people had color printers available to them.)

As the years went on, the companies I worked for changed, and the technology available to trainers progressed at a rapid pace. I started developing eLearning (then known as "CBT" courses) in the late 1990s, eventually moving into web-based training, "rapid development" tools, and eventually online performance support systems.

So, that brings us to the next quickly evolving learning technology—eBooks.

The Past and Future of eBooks

The concept of electronic books has been around for quite some time. Arguably the most widely known digital document format (the Adobe Portable Document Format—or, PDF) was demonstrated by Adobe Systems at Comdex in 1992. However, over twenty years earlier, "Project Gutenberg" had been started by a University of Illinois freshman by the name of Michael Hart.

In July, 1971 Project Gutenberg was born. Named after the fifteenth century man who is considered the father of modern printing, the project was founded with the simple mission "to encourage the creation and distribution of eBooks." Starting with the *United States Declaration of Independence*, Hart (and other volunteers) began the slow process of manually typing the text of public domain documents into a simple ASCII format. In August, 1989 (over 18 years after its founding) Project Gutenberg completed its tenth book, *The King James Bible*. Encompassing both testaments, the digital version of the Bible was around 5MB in size.

However, the advent of the Internet hastened the project's development. With the release of the first true Web browser (Mosaic) in 1993 it became much easier to recruit volunteers and harvest their efforts. Between 1991 and 1996, the number of books in the project doubled every year. In 1997, the thousandth book was added; in 2002 there were 5000; and by October 2003 the collection contained 10,000 documents. As of early 2011, Project Gutenberg contains over 33,000 documents. Every document is in the public domain and available for free download. The project's website is www.gutenberg.org.

One of the first major experiments with commercial eBooks was the release of Stephen King's *Riding the Bullet* in 2000. With over 400,000 copies downloaded within the first twenty four hours of availability, the future of publishing seemed initially evident. However, the technical infrastructure, consumer hardware, and intellectual property protections (now called DRM, or Digital Rights Management) had not yet evolved to the point where commercial eBooks were seriously viable.

Amazon.com was founded in 1995 as one of the first online bookstores. It later expanded into other lines of merchandise, and is today the largest online retailer in the United States. Amazon began selling the Kindle in 2007 which launched the popularity of the eReader as a consumer electronic device. (Although, Amazon did not invent the first eReader. Sony Corporation began selling the Librie eReader device in 2004.) It was the Amazon Kindle that really introduced eReaders to the masses.

In the past few years, many more eReaders have been introduced to market. These include product updates from Amazon and Sony, as well as entries by established booksellers (the Barnes and Noble

"Nook"), and upstarts like the Canadian company Kobo. Even as the eReaders have expanded in popularity and functionality, their prices have dropped significantly.

In addition to dedicated eReaders, many other devices have expanded into the eReader realm. All smartphone models (iPhone, Android, Blackberry, Windows Phones, etc.) and tablet computers (iPad, Galaxy Tab, Motorola Xoom, Blackberry Playbook, etc.) have eReader applications (or "apps") designed for them. And, of course, it's still possible to read eBooks the "old fashioned" way on your desktop or laptop computer!

So, where is the future of eBooks/eReaders heading, and why is it important to those of us in the role of workplace learning and performance? Consider this information:

- eBooks now comprise nearly 10% of all book sales.

- eBook sales are expected to grow by 47% each year until at least 2015 (Goldman Sachs).

- Amazon now sells more eBooks than traditional print; 143 eBooks are sold for every 100 printed books.

- In a 14-nation survey done by Boston Consulting Group (May, 2010), 49% of respondents said they planned to buy an eReader or tablet device within the next three years.

These trends point to continued acceptance and proliferation of eBooks and eReaders, and as such make them a viable alternative for how we create, publish, and distribute learning materials within our organizations.

About this Book

This book is intended for use by learning professionals who want to learn how to publish content in eBook format.

The goal is not only to provide the "nuts and bolts" instructions for creating an eBook, but also to examine the history and future of this medium, and the pros and cons of using it for learning materials.

The book is divided into ten chapters:

Chapter 1: This chapter covers the history of eBooks, and the benefits (or drawbacks) in using eBooks/eReaders for training materials.

Chapter 2: This chapter provides an overview of the most popular models of eReader hardware.

Chapter 3: This chapter looks at the different eBook formats, and talks about the differences and similarities between them.

Chapter 4: This chapter does a deeper dive into the anatomy of the EPUB file format. It is easily the most "technical" chapter of the book. Its purpose here is to provide a deeper understanding of the prevailing eBook format for those who have an interest in understanding the technology. But, if getting deeper into the technology does not appeal to you, feel free to skip on to Chapter 5.

Chapter 5: This chapter provides an overview of the complete workflow you can follow to create an eBook from existing material.

Chapter 6-9: These chapters provide the detailed instructions you will follow to create eBook learning materials. The specific chapters cover creating the content, formatting the document, publishing the eBook, and distributing the final product.

Chapter 10: This chapter is a summary of the material, and provides contact information for the other.

Who is the Audience for this Book?

- This book is written for those people who design and deliver learning. While my background focuses mostly on training and development in a corporate setting, this book is really intended for anyone in the "trainer" or "teacher" role, who wants to learn more about eBooks.

- This book does not require you to be a hard core "techie" or proficient in website building, coding, Flash, or anything similar. We will discuss the more technical topics in simple terms, and will reference user-friendly and inexpensive tools.

- Quite simply, the only prerequisite is that you have an interest in learning about how you can create eBooks for your own learning materials.

CHAPTER 1

What is an eBook?

This chapter will explore the definition of an eBook, and how the format could be applied to learning resources within your organization. It will also look at some pros and cons of this emerging format.

The Trainer as Author & Publisher

Whether you realize it or not, if you develop learning materials, you are an author and a publisher. As we write user guides, training manuals, and other materials we follow the basic tenets of authoring and publishing. That process includes research, draft development, editing, and finally—publishing and distribution. The main difference between professional authors/publishers and learning developers, however, is the learning professional does the whole gamut!

The publishing industry is in the midst of a substantial sea change. The role of publisher as "gatekeeper" is quickly diminishing as publishing options for independents become more viable. These include not only cheaper on-demand options for printed books, but also the ability to publish in eBook formats.

As developers of learning materials, these same new avenues for publishing are available to us as well.

What is an eBook?

According to the *Oxford Companion to the Book* (Oxford Press, 2010) an eBook is defined as "a text and image based publication in digital form produced on, published by, and readable on computers or other devices."

While this definition is certainly encompassing and could apply to nearly every document not printed on paper. For purposes of this book, we will focus on specific eBook formats and reader hardware generally associated with book publication.

The Advantages of eBooks in Learning

So, why would a learning professional consider publishing his or her materials in eBook format? There are some significant advantages to this publishing method.

Mobility

The most significant advantage to an eBook as a learning material format is its mobile nature. Probably more than any other digital format, eBooks were designed to be read on mobile devices, such as Kindles, Nooks, tablet computers, and smart phones. As such, they are easy for learners to read and use on the go.

Ease of Updating Content

Because the format is digital, it is much easier to update and distribute materials than it is with traditionally printed content. A new version can be quickly published, "pushed out" to the learners, and the new version overwrites the previous version on their reading device.

Cost Effective Publication

Unlike traditional printed materials, content developed in eBook format is much less expensive to publish and distribute. While the time and effort it takes to develop the content remains consistent with the traditional formats, there is no cost in the actual production of the material for your learners. In fact, it costs no more to distribute ten thousand "copies" of your material than it does to distribute just one.

A side benefit to the cost effective nature, is the inclination to be more diligent in keeping materials current. Since the cost for re-distribution is not a factor, most developers are more apt to update and publish their materials more frequently.

Multimedia Capability*

One of the emerging characteristics of eBooks is the ability to integrate multimedia elements (video, audio, interactive graphics, etc.) into content. However, you may notice that there is an asterisk marking this particular benefit. That's because currently multimedia content is not an accepted standard within the prevailing format of the moment (EPUB format version 2.0.1). An EPUB with embedded multimedia will not pass a validation check, and therefore may not be eligible for placement in many distribution channels.

However, while the standard may not be currently accepted, it for the most part still works. Most content integrated into eBook source using HTML 5 will work in the majority of eReaders. (This is especially true of the Apple iBooks software which is very "forgiving" in the content it accepts.) So, if you are not planning on distributing your materials through the commercial channels (i.e., the Kindle or Nook bookstores), you may not find this "rule breaking" a deterrent to your publication.

This situation is expected to be resolved when the standards for EPUB version 3.0 are released later in 2011.

eReader "Plusses"

One of the main advantages to publishing in eBook format is the features which are inherent to most (if not all) eReading devices. These features are built into the firmware running the eReader itself, and requires no effort on your part.

Scalable & Re-Flowable Text

One of the biggest advantages of eBooks, especially over other digital formats like PDF, is the ability to change the visual aspects of the text and have the entire document "re-flow" to fit your selected view.

This is a real advantage with text size, since your learners can set the text size which is most readable for them, without having to be concerned with hampering the overall layout of the material.

While text size is the primary consideration, there are other elements which can be specified by the reader based on his or her own preference. This includes specifying a desired typeface (i.e., Arial versus Times New Roman), and the "paper" color. All of these elements can help maximize readability based on what works best for each individual.

Built-In Dictionary

Every major eReader platform contains a built-in dictionary function. This means that every single word within your material can provide a dictionary definition when called by the learner. This requires no additional work on your part such as creating a glossary. This is an automatic feature of the eReader software.

A few of the eReaders will allow you to specify your own dictionary source (or, modify the existing one) in the reader software. This could be helpful for developing your own industry-specific dictionary functions.

Bookmarking

The eReader devices automatically remember how far you have read in a book, and immediately jump to that position the next time the material is opened. In addition, you can bookmark specific passages within the book to quickly jump back to those sections later.

Highlights, Annotations & Notes

All of the eReaders also allow you to highlight passages of interest; make annotations to the materials; and write your own text regarding elements you wish to note. These enhancements are added to the eBook on your device and continue to remain available until the book is deleted.

Disadvantages of eBooks?

For all of their advantages, few methods or formats are perfectly suited for all situations. So, what are some situations that might give you pause before developing your learning material in eBook format?

Lack of Comfort with Digital Reading

While our learners have come a long way in the past decade in their acceptance of giving up the "comfort" of paper-based materials, there are still a good number of students who do not feel comfortable with anything other than the old-fashioned paper "manual."

There is nothing wrong with that. And, by and large this is a generational issue, and we must make content development decisions that work best for the majority of our students. As the instructional designer, you will need to take into consideration the ability of your students to adapt (and hopefully, thrive with) this technology. Regardless of how great the technology is, if your learners will not accept and embrace it, it will become a hinderance— rather than an enhancement—to your learning programs.

Limited Distribution of eReaders

While the popularity of eReaders has skyrocketed over the past two years, the devices are still far from omnipresent. Not every student will have access to an eReader, and that can impact how completely you can utilize this format.

Eventually, you can expect to see eReaders become more and more corporate purchased and supported devices. After all, with the cost of printing, binding, etc. factored in for all the materials produced, it does not take long for a $150 eReader that can hold <u>thousands</u> of pages of learning content to become very cost effective.

Variations in Hardware & Software

The eBook and eReaders are emerging platforms, particularly for publishing learning content. Although there are many advantages to being on the "cutting edge" when taking advantage of these platforms, there are also some risks.

Right now, instead of there being a single unified standard for an eBook file format (as there is, for example, with .DOC for word processing documents, or .PDF for portable printed documents), there are multiple accepted formats for eBooks. While two popular formats have emerged with Mobipocket and EPUB (see Chapter 3 for more details on eBook formats), these are still two major competing formats which bring individual design considerations.

Even with a consistent format (EPUB) there are variations in how different eReader devices will interpret the same book. For example, the iPad/iPhone, Sony Reader, and Barnes & Noble Nook all use the same EPUB format, but your book may encounter variations in how it is displayed on each of those devices.

CHAPTER 2

The Hardware: eReaders

Electronic document formats have been around for several years, but what has really changed the playing field for this format recently is the advent of the portable eReader. This chapter will explore the more popular eReader models currently available, and some of the characteristics that they share.

The Age of the eReader

Probably the most significant element in the rising popularity of eBooks has to do with the new hardware platforms which support the format and have come to market in the past few years. The advent of the "eReader" have given readers (and, in our case—students) the ability to carry their reading material with them so that it is available nearly instantaneously from anywhere they happen to be located.

Small, lightweight, and relatively inexpensive, the eReader has greatly impacted the usability of the eBook format. While it has been possible to read content digitally almost since the very introduction of computers, the cumbersome nature of these machines (desktop or laptop) limited the convenience of digital reading. The introduction (and subsequent popularity) of the eReader has changed that for the better.

This chapter will explore the technology behind the hardware, and some of the currently available popular eReaders. It is important to keep in mind that new reader hardware is introduced almost every week, so this is far from a comprehensive list. However, the readers mentioned here have proven to have some staying power in the market, so these brands will most likely be prominent for some time.

For up-to-date listings and reviews of a variety of eReader hardware, check out the "Mobile Read Wiki" at http://wiki.mobileread.com/wiki/Main_Page/. This is a great online resource for all elements of mobile reading.

Displays: E Ink vs. LCD

Nearly all eReaders display their content using one of two technologies: E Ink or backlit LCD (liquid crystal display). Like most things, both technologies have their strengths and weaknesses.

E Ink is a proprietary technology of a company called E Ink Corporation. E Ink is considered a type of electronic paper, which is a technology class designed to mimic the look of real paper and print on an electronic screen.

E Ink works by suspending millions of microcapsules within a clear liquid. Each microcapsule contains positively charged white particles and negatively charged black particles. When a positive charge is applied, the white particles are pulled to the front of the display where they are visible by the reader. When a negative charge is applied, the black particles are made visible. This switching of positive and negative charges is what causes the readable text to be displayed on the screen.

LCDs also work with electrical charges to create their displays. The terms "liquid" and "crystal" may sound like a contradiction in terms, but liquid crystal does possess characteristics of both liquids and solids. An LCD is comprised of two flat layers of polarized film; a layer of liquid crystal; and a reflective surface behind it all. As the liquid crystals are charged, they change shape which affects how light is reflected off the mirrored surface, and the polarized films control what is visible. The liquid crystals can be displayed at the pixel level, with each pixel being made up of three sub-pixels of red, green, and blue to allow for displayed color variation. LCDs emit no light of their own, so backlighting is used to illuminate the display through the liquid crystal and polarized displays.

So, which display is better? It really depends on your needs and the conditions under which you are using the eReader. E Ink technology works much better in bright light, since light hitting those displays is not reflected back causing glare. An E Ink display can be read in bright sunlight with no negative impact on readability. These displays are also have very low energy requirements; an E Ink display can go for weeks on a single battery charge.

LCD displays, however, allow a much fuller range of display capability, including high definition color images and video. Also, because they are backlit, LCD display can be better used in low-light situations. While the energy efficiency has improved significantly (and continues to improve constantly), the time between charges still does not come close to matching that of E Ink readers.

Connectivity: How do Readers "Talk"?

The main advantage of an eReader is its ability to be easily transported. However, there has to be some easy way to get content loaded onto the devices.

Most current eReaders use either WiFi or cellular 3G service (or, a combination of both) to connect the reading device to content sources. Most readers also usually contain sort of hard-wired connection (usually USB) to a computer to allow content to be transferred.

WiFi only devices tend to be cheaper than those which use 3G. This is because the cost of the cellular service is built into the upfront cost of these devices. Again, the environment in which you will most likely be using the reader should determine which connectivity you need. For example, if you will be using the device in an area without WiFi, a 3G version might be your best option.

Formats: What do they Read?

The next chapter will discuss more about the different formats of eBooks, but it is important to note that different reader devices tend to focus on specific formats. For example, the Amazon Kindle uses a proprietary format based on the Mobipocket standard. The Barnes and Noble Nook and iPad primarily use the EPUB format.

While most content can be "translated" to run on most any device, the devices preferred format should also be considered when choosing a hardware platform.

The eReader Platforms

This book makes no attempt to critically review or recommend any eReader platform over any other; a simple overview of several devices will be covered. Individuals tend to be very brand loyal to their eReader of choice, so the good news is that it is very unlikely you will make a bad choice among the major brands.

The Sony Reader

Sony was the first hardware company to introduce a dedicated eReader to market. Launched in 2005, the Sony Reader was also the first commercially available device to use E Ink technology.

The Sony Reader reads several formats, but is primarily designed for EPUB files. Sony markets a few different versions of the Reader with different features, and frequently upgrades existing models.

Sony offers its own online bookstore, as well as partners with Project Gutenberg and many public library systems to provide content.

The Amazon Kindle

Amazon launched the Kindle in 2007, and is currently on the third generation of hardware. The Kindle is currently only offered with a grey scale E Ink display. It is offered in both a WiFi only version, and combination WiFi/3G.

The Kindle can be credited as the device which really jumpstarted the eReader revolution, and is thought to be the best selling of the devices. (Amazon has said that the Kindle is their best selling item in history—even outselling the final *Harry Potter* book.)

The Kindle uses a DRM (digital rights management) protected proprietary format of MOBI called AZW. The Kindle is the only major eReader not to use (or even recognize) EPUB as its standard format.

Kindle content can be purchased through the Amazon.com online bookstore, and currently provides the largest catalog of eBooks for purchase.

The Barnes & Noble Nook

Released for the 2009 Holiday Season, the Nook was mega-bookseller Barnes and Noble's competitive entry into the eReader market. It is offered in an E Ink display version (in both WiFi only and WiFi/3G), and a color version which uses a backlit LCD display.

The color version is unique in that it runs the open source Android operating system. While marketed as a dedicated eReader device, this variation in its operating system actually puts it closer in definition to a tablet computer than a stand-alone eReader.

The Nook takes advantage of the Barnes and Noble (barnesandnoble.com) online book store for supplying content to the Nook devices.

The Kobo eReader

Offered by the Canadian company Kobo, Inc., the first version of the Kobo eReader was released in May, 2010. It uses an E Ink display, and was originally intended to be the very low cost alternative to the Amazon Kindle. (However, Amazon has since significantly dropped the entry-level price on the Kindle.)

The original version of the Kobo device offered no wireless connectivity, but an updated WiFi-only version was released in October, 2010. Instead of offering its own eReader, the bookstore chain Borders partnered with Kobo to offer its reader device through their stores and website.

The Kobo eReader accesses its own online bookstore, as well as Borders Books website. In addition, it comes pre-loaded with 100 public domain classic books.

The Tablets

A "tablet" is a device that provides many of the same features and functions of a full-computer, but with some limitations. Due to their size and portable nature, tablets have emerged as popular eReader devices.

The segment is probably best defined by Apple's iPad, which launched its first generation in the Spring of 2010. However, in recent months the market has added more tablet devices from major brands (i.e. the Galaxy Tab, the Motorola Xoom, the Blackberry Playbook, etc.), with many more anticipated to enter the market soon.

Most eReader platforms offer programs (called "apps") for the tablet devices. For example, there are eReading apps for Kindle, Nook, Kobo, and many others all available on the iPad. Usually free in cost, these apps allow you to have a variety of eReaders all available within your one tablet device.

Smartphones

A "smartphone" is a cellular phone that provides many of the features of a computer (i.e., internet connectivity). Some of the most popular smartphone platforms include the Apple iPhone, Android phones (software powered by Google, and available on a variety of hardware devices), Blackberry, Microsoft, Palm, and many others.

Like tablet devices, most eReader platforms offer smartphone apps of their reading software. This provides the ability to have a variety of eReaders all available within one smartphone device.

The size of a smartphone is both its best and worst feature as an eReader. Being pocket-sized, it is incredibly light and portable.

However, the screen size (usually around four to five inches) makes it difficult for some people to use as a reading device.

CHAPTER 3

The Software: eBook Formats

As a relatively new technology, the standards are still developing regarding eBook formats. This chapter will discuss the various file formats.

eReaders Require Content

The previous chapter focused on some specifics about eReader hardware, and provided an overview of some popular platforms. However, eReader hardware has no use without eBook formatted software.

As is typically the case with emerging platforms, a few different eBook formats have evolved and are competing for supremacy.

While there are specific file types which are considered true eBook formats, the spectrum of available formats for digital text is quite extensive. This book breaks down the various digital text formats into four categories:

- Text Document Formats

- Mark-Up Language Formats

- Portable Document Format

- eBook Formats

The Text Document Formats

Digital text has been around since the early days of personal computing. One of oldest formats is the .TXT (text) file type. Often referred to as "plain text", this format contains only alphanumeric characters, punctuation, and special characters but with no special formatting (i.e., boldface, italics, etc.) possible.

The .TXT format evolved into a more advanced type called Rich Text Format (.RTF). The .RTF format also contains alphanumeric characters, punctuation, and special characters but does allow special formatting such as boldface, italics, and underlining.

The Microsoft Word document format (.DOC or .DOCX) is a proprietary word processing format that has become so pervasive in its popularity that it is recognized as a nearly universal digital text format.

Mark-Up Language Formats

The "mark-up" languages are best represented by the Hypertext Mark-Up Language (HTML) and Extensible Mark-Up Language (XML). These formats are the language of the World Wide Web.

HTML is an alphanumeric character set which uses "tags" to turn on and off formatting. These tags are translated into a viewable format by web browser software. For example, to display the HTML code Title would appear to a reader in a web browser as **Title**.

XML is designed for structuring data which is interpreted and read by a target device (like a web browser). XML often works in conjunction with HTML to structure and display information within web pages. XML also uses tags (although, for a different purpose than HTML). The most prevalent current eBook standard (EPUB) also uses XML to structure book data.

Since literally millions of pages of information are listed on the Internet using the mark-up languages, we include them here with the other digital text formats.

Portable Document Format

The Portable Document Format (PDF) is a digital publishing format created and owned by Adobe Systems Corporation. The PDF was announced by Adobe in the early 1990s, and over the next decade became the prominent digital publishing format.

The format displays documents independent of the authoring software used to create them. A PDF includes complete information about each document, including its text, typefaces, images, layout and any other information needed to display it matching the author's original design.

The PDF file type was originally a proprietary format of Adobe, but it was released as an open standard in July, 2008. This open standard is published by the International Organization for Standardization (the governing body which publishes the ISO standards). The move to an open standard greatly increased the PDF's popularity as a digital document format, and allowed other software manufacturers to design their applications to "print" in PDF format.

Even without the ability to reformat and reflow based on the reader device, PDFs have remained a very popular format for publishing eBooks. The majority of eBook readers (including the Kindle, Nook, and iPad) have the ability to display PDF files.

eBook Formats

What distinguishes the eBook formats from the previously listed document types is that these formats were built specifically for use on eReaders.

There are many file formats which can be considered eBook specific, but this chapter will focus on the few which have gained (and are maintaining) the largest representation. A complete guide to all eBook formats can be found on the "Mobile Read Wiki" at http://wiki. mobileread.com/wiki/Main_Page/.

Mobipocket

The Mobipocket (.mobi) format was originally a product of a French company called Mobipocket, SA and was incorporated to produce Mobipocket Reader software, an eBook reader for PDAs, phones, and desktop operating systems. Mobipocket was purchased by Amazon in 2005.

The .mobi format is a highly compressed database driven format that is ideal for portable devices. From a technical construction standpoint it is very similar to the EPUB format, with the main difference being that Mobipocket is a proprietary format (owned by Amazon) while EPUB is an open source format.

There are a few variations of the Mobipocket standard that are represented by other eBook formats.

.AZW

The .AZW format is used by Amazon specifically for the Kindle eReader. The format is essentially identical to the Mobipocket standard, with a slight difference in how it records document serial numbers and it uses its own DRM formatting. All of the books sold via the Amazon Kindle bookstore are in .AZW format.

While most eReaders will read the Mobipocket format in addition to

EPUB, the Kindle is unique it that it will only read Mobipocket format eBooks (excluding, of course PDF files which for our purposes we do not actually classify as an eBook format, but rather its own unique digital publication type). Because of the popularity of the Kindle device (it is generally considered the best selling eReader), eBooks in Mobipocket format hold a very large percentage of all eBooks sold and distributed.

.PRC

The file extension .PRC stands for Palm Resource Compiler, and is usually associated with devices running the Palm OS. As an eBook format, the .PRC is identical to the Mobipocket format. (In fact, you can rename a file.prc to file.mobi with no impact on the readability of the eBook file.)

The difference is that the .PRC file format is more wide ranging—it can contain a Mobipocket eBook, or it could contain some completely unrelated thing, since the .PRC at its most basic level only means that it is a Palm OS application container.

EPUB

The format EPUB stands for "electronic publication" and is a free and open eBook standard supported by the International Digital Publishing Forum (IDPF). Books published in this format carry the .EPUB file extension.

The EPUB format is the primary eBook document type for several of the most popular eReaders, including the Barnes and Noble Nook, Sony Reader, Kobo eReader, and the iPad/iPhone. The major exception is the Amazon Kindle which does not read the EPUB format.

The EPUB is technically very similar to the .MOBI/.AZW format, except that is a slightly less compressed file. In addition, the EPUB provides more flexibility in layout and formatting, providing the ability to do things like drop caps and text wrapping.

Due to its free and open nature, and that fact that it is considered an international standard, the EPUB has become a very popular eBook format. Sometimes referred to as "the MP3 of eBooks," we will examine the EPUB format in greater detail in the next chapter.

CHAPTER 4

Anatomy of an EPUB

Often called "the MP3 of eBooks," what exactly makes up the design of an EPUB file? This chapter will dig a little deeper into how an EPUB is constructed.

Overview of the EPUB Format

The eBook format called EPUB is short for "electronic publication" and is the free and open eBook standard supported by the International Digital Publishing Forum (IDPF). Books in this format are named with a file extension of .EPUB.

The EPUB format became the official standard of the IDPF in September 2007, and it replaced an older standard called Open eBook (OEB).

The current version of the EPUB standard is v2.0.1 and was released in May, 2010. A working group within the IDPF has been convened to develop standards for EPUB v3.0. The new version of the standard is expected to improve the functionality of the EPUB format. The working committee issued a draft of the new standard in February, 2011, with the new standard expected to be published later in 2011. Detailed information about the EPUB 3.0 project can be found at http://idpf.org/epub/30/.

EPUB Features

The IDPF lists the following as features of the EPUB format:

- Free and open use of the format;

- Reflowable (word wrapping) and resizable text;

- Inline raster and vector images;

- Embedded metadata;

- DRM (Digital Rights Management) support;

- Cascading Style Sheet (CSS) styling;

- Support for alternative renditions within the same file; and

- Use of inline and out-of-line XML to extend EPUB functionality

Mechanics of the EPUB

An EPUB file is actually a zipped archive containing a multiple hierarchical file structure. Each of the folders and files in the structure has a specific naming convention which the eReader device needs to properly interpret the document.

Since this book is not designed for those with a mastery of coding in HTML, XML, and CSS, we will provide a high-level overview of the structure of an EPUB without getting too deeply into the technical details. If you are interested in diving deeper into the technology, the IDPF's web site (http://idpf.org) contains detailed documents on all of the technical specifications of the EPUB format.

EPUB Specifications

The EPUB format consists of three specifications:

- Open Publication Structure (OPS) 2.0 (formatting of the content)

- Open Packaging Format (OPF) 2.0 (the structure of the document in XML)

- OEBPS Container Format (OCF) 1.0 (packages all files in a ZIP archive)

In the most simple terms, the EPUB uses XHTML (or in some cases, DTBook which is another XML standard provided by the DAISY Consortium) to handle the text and structure of the book's content. It uses a sub-set of CSS to derive the layout and formatting, and XML to write the document's manifest (list of files), table-of-contents, and metadata. Lastly, the entire file structure is bundled together in a single compressed file (with a .epub extension) that can be distributed to and read by eReaders.

The three specifications listed above are how the reference information on the IDPF web site is organized.

EPUB File Contents

You can view the contents of an EPUB file simply by renaming it from *bookname*.epub to *bookname*.zip, then opening the ZIP file in any extraction utility application.

The EPUB will typically contain the following folder and file structure:

- mimetype file

- META-INF folder (contains the container.xml file)

- OPBPS folder (contains the books content, formatting, table-of-contents, metadata, etc.)

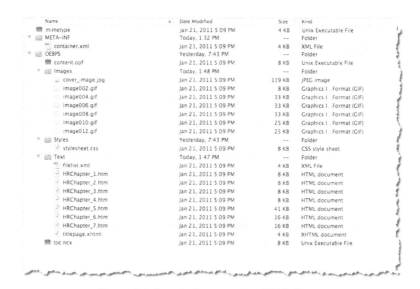

Figure 4.1: Sample Contents of an EPUB File

In the following sections, we will examine each component of the file structure in more detail.

The mimetype File

The mimetype file is very important because it tells the eReader or operating system that this is an EPUB file. It is a simple ASCII text file that contains only one line:

```
application/epub+zip
```

This should be the very first file in the ZIP archive, and should not be altered.

The META-INF Folder

This folder contains the **container.xml** file. This file tells the eReader software where to find the **content.opf** file, which in turn lists all of the book's content structure information. The META-INF folder and container.xml file are identical in every EPUB document.

The OEBPS Folder

This folder is very important, since it contains all of the book's content and layout information.

The **content.opf** file in this folder contains a list of all files in the EPUB; defines their order; and stores the book's metadata (title, author, publisher, ISBN, genre, edition, etc.) information.

The **Images** folder contains any images used in the document. The image formats PNG, JPEG, GIF, and SVG are supported by the EPUB standard.

The **Styles** folder contains the stylesheet used to control the book's formatting. The style sheet is a limited sub-set of the Cascading Style Sheet (CSS) web standard. Specifics of the supported CSS features can be found on the IDPF web site.

The **Text** folder contains the XML, XHTML and HTML files which make up the content of your book. In essence, this is the part you have actually "written."

The **toc.ncx** file contains the books table-of-contents. This file contains navigation links to the applicable content of your book.

CHAPTER 5

Producing an eBook: Workflow

Producing an eBook requires an understanding of the necessary workflow. This chapter will provide an overview of that workflow, and subsequent chapters will focus on the details.

Workflow at a Glance

The workflow for creating and publishing an eBook can best be explained by the following image.

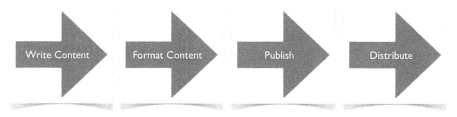

Figure 5-1: Illustrated eBook Workflow

Workflow Overview

Chapters 6-9 will cover the workflow steps in more detail, but this section provides a brief overview of each of the steps.

Write Content

This step covers the actual development, writing, and editing of your learning content. This process can be done specifically to create your eBook, or it could also include the re-purposing of existing learning materials from another format (i.e., a student workbook) to the eBook format.

Format Content

The standards for what can be displayed (and how it is displayed) in an eReader is very exacting. For that reason, we must prepare the format of our content so that it can most easily be translated to the eBook format.

Publish

This step involves the actual conversion of your content to the eBook format, and all of its required technical "packaging." In this step, we will use two excellent (and free!) shareware applications to achieve this process.

Distribute

After your learning content has been successfully published in eBook format, you will need a method to distribute it to your students. In this step we will explore various distribution methods.

CHAPTER 6

Creating the Content

Before you can publish your first eBook, you need to write the content. This chapter will cover the information you need to do about creating content that will eventually end up being your eBook.

Creating Content: The Basics

The best part about creating original content for your eBook is that your writing process does not have to differ from what you have always done. You can continue to use any of the authoring tools for which you are familiar and comfortable.

The only requirement for an authoring tool is that you are able to save your content document as a simple HTML file. Pretty much any writing tool you may be using should have this ability.

New or Existing Content?

Your eBook can either be created from newly written content, or from existing material. This book assumes that many learning professionals reading this will have a need to convert a library of existing material to eBook format.

To convert existing material, the only real requirement is that you have a digital file of the content. Ideally, that file should be in the format of the original authoring tool (i.e., Word, InDesign, etc.). While its possible to deconstruct a PDF of the content (if that's all you have), it is a much easier process if you have the original source file.

If you are writing the content as an eBook from the start, you may actually want to consider developing the material directly in the Sigil eBook publication software. We will talk a lot more about Sigil in Chapter Eight.

Working with Various Tools

As previously stated, you can author the content of a eBook with pretty much any tool you would like to use. However, you do not need to limit yourself to the "traditional" tools which most frequently come to mind (i.e., Word).

This section will look at some different methods you could use to develop your original content that could follow the workflow to become eBooks.

Word Processors

One of the first authoring tool categories which come to mind is that of the many available word processors. The only requirement is that your word processor is able to save the document as a simple HTML file.

Here are some of the common word processing applications many learning developers may be using:

- Microsoft Word
- Apple iWork Pages
- Adobe Framemaker
- Word Perfect

In addition to these full-featured word processing applications, you could also use a simple text editing program, such as Notepad (Windows) or TextEdit (Mac). Remember, the goal is to get to a simple HTML version of your content. All of the special formatting can be done later in the eBook publication tool.

Page Layout Applications

If you are converting materials to eBook which have previously been published, it is possible that the original source files may be in one of the more full-featured page layout/desktop publishing applications.

Some of these common page layout tools include:

- Adobe PageMaker
- Adobe InDesign
- Quark
- Microsoft Publisher

Web Page Development Tools

Because our goal is to end up with a simple HTML document, using any of the popular web page authoring tools could also be a good candidate for developing eBook content. This is especially true if a lot of your existing material is in the form of intranet-based web pages.

While there are many web page editors available (both open source and paid versions), here are a few examples:

- Adobe DreamWeaver

- Microsoft Expression Web (previously called FrontPage)

- Apple iWeb

- Amaya (open source)

Performance Support Development Tools

Another possible path for repurposing existing content into eBooks could include performance support materials. "Performance support" is a larger category of learning materials which could include things like online help and online demos.

Adobe RoboHelp

RoboHelp is a tool for developing online help which been a popular authoring platform for over a decade. RoboHelp contains a feature which allows you to publish a complete help system as a Word-based user guide. This resulting Word file can then be processed down into a simple HTML file which can be migrated to eBook format.

Adobe Captivate

While the most common use for the Captivate tool is to create software-based demos and simulations, it also includes a feature which allows you to publish a demo as text based "how to" document in Word format. This resulting Word document can then be processed down into a simple HTML file which can be migrated into eBook format.

CHAPTER 7

Formatting the eBook

Prior to converting your book to the EPUB format, you need to make sure the formatting is as "clean" as possible to enable a smooth conversion process. This chapter will talk about how to format your content.

Why Format? I Like the Way it Looks!

If you are working to convert existing learning material to eBook format, chances are you are already pretty happy with its look and format. So, why would we want to remove the formatting as part of the eBook conversion process?

The simple answer is that formatting that lends itself to printed materials (or even PDFs) may not translate well when converted to eBook. Since the layout of an eBook can re-flow based on the reader's preferences, a heavily formatted document many not display well for all readers. Simple formatting (using associated stylesheets) generally works best for eBooks.

Smashwords Style Guide

Smashwords.com is an eBook publishing and distribution platform for authors, publishers, and readers. It is the leading eBook publishing platform for independent authors and publishers with over 40,000 books published by over 16,000 authors & publishers.

Smashwords is a free service for authors and publishers, and hosts its own online bookstore for readers. In addition, Smashwords acts as a book aggregator and distributes eBooks to many of the major eBookstores, including Barnes and Noble, Kobo, Diesel, Sony, and the Apple iBooks store. If you have any interest in publishing your eBook to a public audience, Smashwords.com provides an excellent opportunity to make that happen.

One of the books that Smashwords offers on their site is their free Style Guide which explains how to format your content so that it can be converted to an eBook to be used on their sites and partner stores.

Even if you do not plan to publish on Smashwords.com, the Style Guide can be a fantastic resource when converting your own book. It offers a great, simple, step-by-step guide to how to properly format your eBook.

I highly recommend downloading this free resource from the Smashwords.com web site.

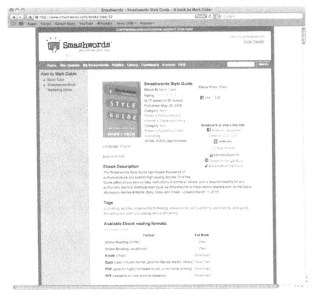

Figure 7-1: The Smashwords Style Guide Download Page

Tools for Formatting

Our goal is to convert our existing content into something that will convert easily (and well) to the EPUB format. Chapter 8 will walk through the process of actually converting the document to EPUB.

The tools we use for formatting the content can vary, just like the tools we used originally to write the content. For example, Adobe InDesign CS5 contains a very robust EPUB export engine and will automatically convert your original content to a workable EPUB. (Although, an EPUB that may still require some "tweaking" before distribution.)

In our example, we are going to assume that Microsoft Word was used to create our original content (or was written in a tool that can easily convert to Word or RTF). In this scenario, we will format our Word document and export it as a simple HTML file which can later be converted to EPUB.

Document Formatting Guidelines

This section contains an overview of the basics of good formatting at this point in our process. Again, I suggest you download the free

Smashwords Style Guide for an excellent step-by-step resource.

Save Your Work Under a New File Name

This is probably a simple concept for most people, but is important to mention here. Do not do the reformatting work on your original file; instead, save it under a different name so that your original file remains safe and unaltered.

Turn on the Show/Hide Feature

By turning on Word's show/hide feature you can clearly see the document's current formatting, including things like spaces and paragraph returns. This feature is toggled on and off by clicking the "paragraph" (or "backward P")button on the formatting toolbar. (The technical term for this character in typography is called a "pilcrow.")

Turn Off AutoCorrect & AutoFormat

By default, Word tries to assist you by autocorrecting things it believes you have done in error. It also tries to guess what formatting you want as you write. While that may be helpful when creating normal documents, this sort of "help" when formatting for eBook conversion can be a hinderance. These automatic features should be turned off before you begin formatting.

Eliminate Text Boxes

Text boxes are used to contain text to a certain area of the page, which can be great for the printed page or PDF. However, since eBooks reflow content based on reader options, they are problematic for eBooks.

Convert all text boxes to normal text. This will probably require you to "cut" the text out of the existing box, delete the box, then paste the text inline.

Remove Styles & Normalize Text

Because the eBook conversion process cannot always properly convert or recognize applied styles, I usually remove them at this point in the process. (In Word, I would select all the text and set the style as "Normal.") However, we will reestablish text styles in the eBook publication tool (Chapter 8).

Character-based formatting (things like boldface, underline, italics, etc.) tend to translate without much trouble, so you can leave them in your content.

Remove Page & Section Breaks

Forced page and section breaks will not be recognized by the eBook format (again, because they are designed to reflow based on the reader), so it is best to remove them.

Images

Images should be embedded within your content (as opposed to linked), so that they will be maintained during the conversion process.

Images should be placed in-line (not floating). Floating images may appear in unpredictable places after conversion.

Other Items to Consider

Here are some other items to avoid/consider when formatting for your eBook:

- Avoid excessive paragraph returns (this can result in blank pages when converted to eBook).

- Do not use "spaces" to control text placement. (While it may look ok on your screen, it almost never converts properly.)

- Avoid exotic fonts (it's best to stick with the "normal" typefaces: Times, Helvetica, Arial, Garamond, etc.)

- Avoid text in tables, since they do not convert well to eBook. If you have information in tabular format, bring it in as an image.

- Do not put text in columns (again, not supported in eBook formats).

Saving the Formatted File

After completing all the necessary formatting work (which, can be quite a long process depending on the size of your document), we will save the completed file as a simple HTML file. The HTML file will then be converted to EPUB format by another application (see Chapter 8).

You should select to **Save entire file into HTML**.

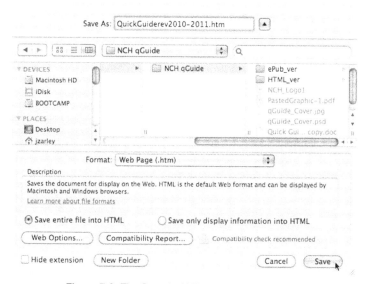

Figure 7-2: The Save As HTML Dialog in Microsoft Word

The resulting saved file will contain an HTML (or .HTM) document containing the text of your content. As part of the HTML conversion, a secondary folder will be created containing any images contained in your source document. You will need to keep the resulting HTML file and this auxiliary folder together in the same hierarchy as created by your authoring tool. This will avoid broken image links in the HTML file (and your subsequent eBook).

CHAPTER 8

Publishing the eBook

This chapter covers the process of converting the document into EPUB format, appropriately formatting it, and readying it for distribution. This chapter will also introduce some great open source tools for eBook publication.

Overview of the Publication Process

This chapter covers the most important part of our overall workflow, because this is the point at which we convert the document into an EPUB file, and format it to appropriately display in eReader devices.

Specifically, we will cover these three steps:

- Creating the eBook Cover
- Covert our source document to EPUB; and
- Layout and format the book for readers.

Creating the eBook Cover

The eBook cover is an image that will represent your final book. The cover is important, because it is the image that will be displayed to the student on the eReader device's "book shelf." So, a cover image which clearly identifies your book's topic or purpose is valuable.

The cover can be created in any graphic design/editing software tool you would like to use (i.e., Photoshop, Gimp, Paint, etc.) as long as it supports RGB images and allows you to save image files in PNG, GIF, or JPG formats.

When designing your cover image, keep the following points in mind:

- The ideal image size is 600 pixels wide by 900 pixels tall.
- The image must be created in RGB color mode (not CMYK or any other color profile).
- Save the final image in either PNG, GIF, or JPG format.
- Make sure the file size is not too large (smaller files display faster). If your cover image is 500 KB (or larger) you should look for ways to reduce the file size.

Converting to EPUB

In Chapter 7 we formatted the content document to be as simple as possible to remove any issues which could complicate the conversion to EPUB. We will now take the simplified file and convert it to a .epub file format.

This can be accomplished by either converting the file directly out of our authoring tool (if your authoring tool supports this functionality), or by converting our document to a simple HTML format then using an open source tool called Calibre to convert it.

Conversion within the Authoring Tool

With the popularity of eBooks increasing, several popular word processing and desktop publishing tools have added EPUB conversion to their functionality. In cases where the conversion utility has not been built into the base tool, third party solutions have been developed.

Microsoft Word

The most current version of Microsoft Word (version 2010 for PC, or 2011 for Mac) does not offer native EPUB conversion. However, several third party plug-ins are available which will offer this functionality.

A quick web search using the term "Word EPUB conversion" will provide a long list of options. Keep in mind that most of these third party tools are sold at an additional cost, and are not usually supported by Microsoft as part of Word's core functionality.

Open Office

Open Office is an open source community-supported office productivity suite, which offers support for word processing, spreadsheets, presentations, and graphics. Open Office offers much of the functionality of other popular office suites, but is non-profit and free for use.

Since Open Office is community supported, many developers have published extensions which add additional functionality—including EPUB conversion. Consult the Open Office site (www.openoffice.org) for available extensions.

Apple iWork Suite

Apple publishes its own office productivity suite for the Mac. It consists of three separate applications called Pages (word processing), Numbers (spreadsheet), and Keynote (presentation). In addition to the version offered for Mac computers, Apple also offers versions of all three applications designed for the iPad tablet.

The latest version of Pages for the MacOS (iWork '09) contains built in functionality for converting native Pages documents (or MS Word documents or RTF files opened in Pages) to the EPUB file format.

The functionality is available under the **File > Export** menu, and allows you to directly export the document in EPUB format.

Figure 8-1: EPUB Export Dialog in iWork Pages

Adobe InDesign

Adobe has long been a major influence in desktop publishing, and have continued this in their products in the evolution of digital publishing. Adobe InDesign CS5 includes a robust EPUB export feature.

From the **File** menu, select to **Export for EPUB** to convert the document from the native (.indd) InDesign file format to EPUB.

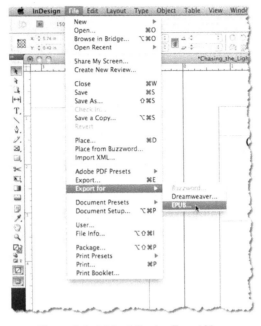

Figure 8-2: Adobe InDesign Export Menu

Instead of just simply converting the file to EPUB format, InDesign provides additional functionality in the export process for tweaking metadata, image representation, and the resulting EPUB's table-of-contents information.

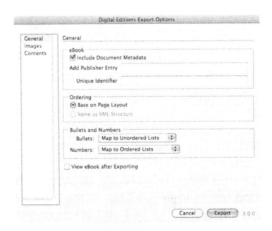

Figure 8-3: Adobe InDesign EPUB Export Options

In addition to the EPUB conversion functionality built into InDesign, Adobe also distributes a (free) companion stand-alone application called Adobe Digital Editions which is used for managing eBook libraries. We will talk more about Digital Editions in the chapter on eBook distribution.

Conversion using Calibre

One of the outstanding open source eBook applications currently available is called Calibre. Calibre is available for free download at http://calibre-ebook.com. Calibre is described as a full eBook management solution, and offers the following features:

- eBook library management;

- eBook conversion;

- Syncing to eReader devices;

- Downloading news from the web and converting it to eBook format;

- Full eBook viewer/reader; and

- Content server for online access to your book.

We will discuss some of the other features of Calibre in the chapter on eBook distribution, but in this section we will focus on its eBook conversion capability.

Convert Content Document to HTML

The first step in using Calibre to convert your document to EPUB format is to convert it to HTML ("web page") format within your authoring tool. Virtually all authoring tools will enable you to save a document in HTML format.

Please note the following important points:

- Convert the content document to HTML, after the format has been simplified (see Chapter 7).

- Select to save your entire document as one HTML file.

- As part of the HTML conversion, a secondary folder will be created containing any images contained in your source document. You will need to keep the resulting HTML file and this auxiliary folder together in the same hierarchy as created by your authoring tool. This will avoid broken image links in the HTML file (and your subsequent eBook).

Download Calibre

The Calibre software is offered for free download at http://calibre-ebook.com. Versions are available for the Windows/PC, Apple Mac, and Linux operating system platforms.

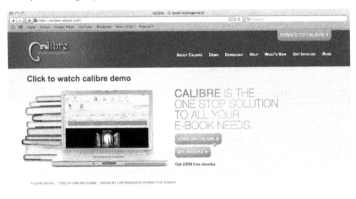

Figure 8-4: The Calibre Home Page

Open the HTML Content in Calibre

After downloading and installing Calibre, you will open the HTML file created from your content document in the original authoring tool. Remember, it is important to keep the HTML file and any folders containing document image folders in the same relationship structure as created during the authoring tool's HTML conversion process.

Within Calibre, click the **Add Books** icon on the toolbar. In the resulting dialog window, select to add books of the HTML file type.

Figure 8-5: Opening the Content HTML File in Calibre

The selected HTML file will be loaded into the Calibre eBook management application.

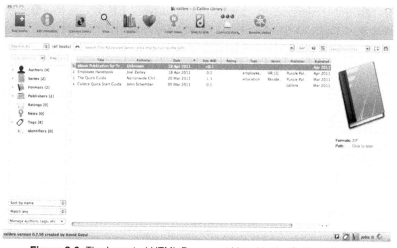

Figure 8-6: The Imported HTML Document Listed in the Calibre Libary

Convert the file to EPUB Format

Converting the imported HTML content document to EPUB is a simple process. With your document selected (highlighted) in the library, click the **Convert Books** icon in the toolbar.

Figure 8-7: The File Conversion Window

In the resulting file conversion window, select **EPUB** as the **Output format** selection in the top-right of the window. Click the **OK** button to convert the document to EPUB format.

The Calibre tool offers additional options in the conversion window for further refining how the eBook is displayed by eReader devices. However, in our example we will do all of the formatting and layout specifications within the publishing tool (Sigil), we will not use that functionality here.

Later, after you have finalized the final version of your eBook in the editing and layout tool, you can come back to this step to convert the eBook into other formats (such as, MOBI for viewing on the Amazon Kindle device). You would just import your final EBUB version back into Calibre (the version we have in Calibre now will be changed significantly once we begin working in the publication tool) and specify the new output format as MOBI.

Specifying Metadata and Book Cover Image

After converting the HTML source document to eBook format, you can now begin adding the specifics (like metadata and the cover image), which uniquely identify it as an eBook.

"Metadata" is defined as data that serves to provide context or additional information about other data. For example, metadata in a eBook can include information such as the publisher, subject, author, etc. The metadata is embedded as part of the book's information.

In the eBook Publication section we will discuss more specifics about eBook metadata using the Sigil tool. However, I find it helpful to specify some basic metadata in Calibre so that it is available immediately upon conversion to EPUB. In addition, I find the Calibre tool and this point in the process also the best opportunity to specify the cover image.

With your content document selected (highlighted), click the Edit Metadata icon on the toolbar.

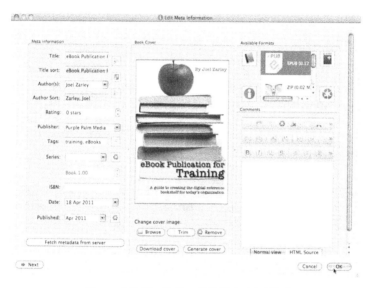

Figure 8-8: The Calibre Edit Metadata Window

From the resulting window, you can specify important elements of the book's metadata (title, author, publisher, search tags, etc.) and embed the book cover image you created earlier.

When you have finished entering the appropriate information, click the **OK** button to return to the library page.

Figure 8-9: Content Document in Library with added Metadata & Cover Image

Note that the metadata information and the cover image you selected is now indicated in the content document's listing in the library.

Saving the EPUB to Your Computer

Right now, our newly converted EPUB file exists only within the Calibre library. So, the last step we need to do in the conversion process is save it to our computer as a .epub file so that we can open it in the publication tool to work with it further.

With the document selected (highlighted) in the library, click the **Save to disk** icon on the toolbar.

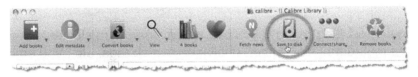

Figure 8-10: The "Save to disk" icon on the toolbar

You will then be asked to specify a location/folder to save the file. The file name automatically defaults to the same name as your original HTML content document.

Layout & Format the Book

Now that we have prepared our content for eBook conversion, and have converted it to EPUB format in Calibre, the last step is to finalize the design, layout and formatting, so that it displays in eReading devices the way we want it to.

This process is made considerably easier by another free and open source tool called Sigil. Sigil is an open source application described as a WYSIWYG ("what you see is what you get") eBook editor. While the content of any eBook can be edited using any text editor, this is really only a viable option if the author is comfortable working in HTML and XML code. Sigil solves that issue by allowing the author to edit eBooks based on the way a reader would actually see them, as opposed to within the raw source code.

This section is not intended to be a comprehensive guide to using Sigil, but rather to include the information you may find most helpful when converting your learning materials to EPUB format. Consult the Sigil project's web site for more information on the tool's functionality.

Download & Install Sigil

The Sigil tool is available as a free download at:

http://code.google.com/p/sigil.

Versions are available for the Windows/PC, Apple Mac, and Linux operating system platforms.

Figure 8-11: The Sigil Download Page

Opening & Working with EPUB Files

When you first launch the Sigil tool it will open with a blank EPUB document displayed.

Figure 8-12: The Sigil Starting Page (Blank File)

To open the EPUB file that was created from our original learning content, click the **Open** icon in the toolbar. Navigate to the .epub file you saved previously and select to open it.

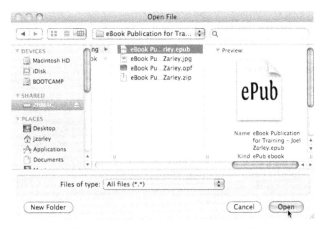

Figure 8-13: Opening the Previously Converted EPUB in Sigil

The User Interface

The Sigil user interface is divided between a Book Browser panel on far left; a large document content area to the right of the Book Browser; and two rows of toolbars along the top.

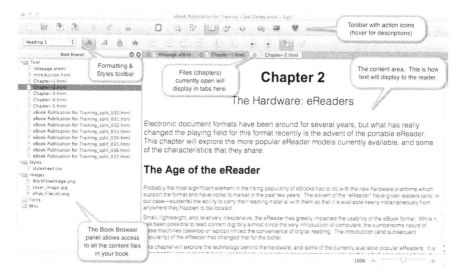

Figure 8-14: The Sigil User Interface

The default content view is in **Reader View**. However, you can select to view the content in **Code View**, which displays the source XML/ HTML code. You can also view the content in **Split View**, which displays the WYSIWIG version at the top, and the corresponding source code view in a split plane below it. Associated buttons on the toolbar allow you to toggle between these three different views.

Figure 8-15: Looking at Content in Code View

Editing the eBook Content

Text editing within the Sigil tool is pretty much the same as it is in any text editor or word processor. Using standard functions (highlighting, copying, pasting, etc.) edit the text so it displays in the format you desire to present to the reader. As you modify the content in the WYSIWYG environment, the code "behind the scenes" is automatically changed to match your edits.

Modifying Content Information

To modify the contents of any text files, double-click the file name to load it into the content pane. From there, you can edit the content just as you would in any word processing application. See the sections on styles and graphics below for more information.

Sometimes the EPUB conversion process splits the text content into multiple files which may not be representative of how you want your final document to look. (For example, it may place a chapter title in its own file, then the content of that chapter as its own subsequent file.) This is a relatively simple (if not somewhat time consuming) task. Simply cut and paste between the chapters to end up with the desired result.

Removing Chapters

You can delete a chapter you no longer need in your book (for example, its content is empty because you have moved the content into other files). To delete a chapter file (or, really any other file type in the Book Browser) you can:

- Select (highlight) it and press the <Delete> key on your keyboard; or

- Right-click on the file and select Remove from the pop-up menu.

Regardless of the method, Sigil will always alert you before it deletes the file.

Figure 8-16: File Delete Alert Message

Adding Chapters

Sometimes you may need to add additional chapters to your book. This can occur when you need to split content from one chapter file into multiple chapters, or if you need to add new (additional) content to your book.

To split an existing chapter into multiple chapters, position your text cursor at the appropriate location and select **Chapter Break** from the **Insert** menu. This will split any content from the cursor forward into its own chapter file.

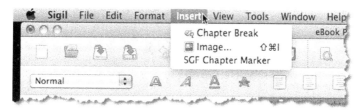

Figure 8-17: The Insert Menu

You may also need to add new content to the EPUB that was not part of your original document. You can do this by either writing the new content directly within Sigil, or by importing an existing content file into the EPUB.

To write the new content directly in Sigil, right-click anywhere in the file area and select **Add New Item** from the pop-up menu. This will add a new file to Book Browser list. Double-click the new file to open it in the content window (which will initially be empty) and write the content.

To import an existing file into the EPUB, select **Add Existing Items...** from the pop-up menu. A dialog window will display to allow you to browse for the appropriate file on your computer. You can add files in either HTML or TXT format. (Content added in HTML will be added to the "Text" folder; files in TXT format will be placed in the "Misc" folder.)

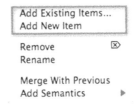

Figure 8-18: Pop-Up Menu with Add Items Options Highlighted

Inserting Graphics

To insert a graphic into the text of your eBook, position the cursor at the desired insertion for the image (this generally works best on an empty line). Then, select **Image...** from the **Insert** menu. (See *Figure 8-17* earlier.)

The image will be inserted into the selected point in your text. In addition, the image file itself will be saved to the **Images** folder within the EPUB file structure.

The EPUB format supports the following graphic file types: PNG, JPG, GIF, and SVG.

Styles & Stylesheets

We removed all of the styling from our original document in Chapter Seven to ensure a clean conversion to EPUB. Now comes the time to reestablish formatting so our final document appears to readers as we desire.

Applying the styles within the Sigil tool will ensure that the styles are integrated into the EPUB file, and as such properly interpreted by the eReading device.

Specifying a Text Style

To apply a style to text, select (highlight) the desired text, then select the appropriate style type from styles list drop-down menu.

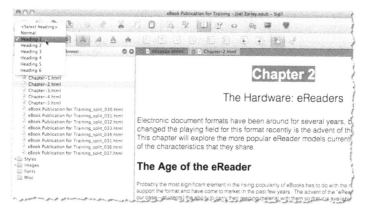

Figure 8-19: Applying a Style to Selected Text

Working with the Stylesheet

The specifics of the individual styles are based on the Cascading Style Sheet (CSS) file contained within the EPUB structure. The CSS is included as part of the conversion to EPUB, and is generally derived from the conversion process used. (For example, we used the Calibre tool to convert our document to EPUB, so our initial style sheet was the default one used by Calibre.)

You can edit the current stylesheet, or bring in a new external CSS into the EPUB structure. To edit the existing stylesheet, double-click the CSS file entry in the **Styles** folder in the Book Browser. The stylesheet's information will load into the content pane.

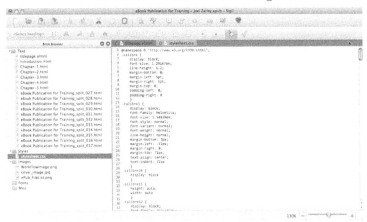

Figure 8-20: The CSS Displayed

With the stylesheet displayed, you can make any edits or modifications necessary. When finished, save the file and any changes you have made will become part of the EPUB's stylesheet.

You can also import in an existing CSS file to use in the EPUB. To import in an existing stylesheet, right-click within the **Styles** folder in the Book Browser and select **Add existing items...** from the pop-up menu. (See *Figure 8-18* as a reference.) Then, browse to find the desired CSS file on your computer. Any CSS file imported into the EPUB will automatically be saved to the **Styles** folder. You may also want to delete the original stylesheet to avoid confusion.

If you are converting a catalog of learning content into eBook format, you may find it very helpful to create an external CSS file that can be applied to all of your content. This will help ensure your learning materials look consistent, and will be a timesaver during eBook publication.

There are many available resources online for learning to write basic stylesheets. You can use any text editor to create a CSS, but web authoring applications (such as Adobe Dreamweaver) work particularly well for this task.

Keep in mind that the EPUB format currently supports a sub-set of the CSS standard—not all CSS functionality is available for use in an eBook. Details about the supported CSS standards in EPUB can be found on the IDPF website.

Working with eBook Mechanics

The are some additional functions we can use to improve the experience our learners have using our eBooks.

Adding Semantics

"Semantics" can be added to XHTML content files and images. They essentially allow you to tag content in the book as having special characteristics, such as an index, glossary, preface, etc. If the student's eReader supports semantic information it can display the tagged content when selected.

To add a semantic tag, right-click on a content file and select **Add Semantics** from the pop-up menu. From the resulting sliding menu, select the appropriate semantic tag.

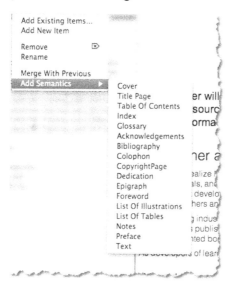

Figure 8-21: Adding Semantics to Content

Working with Metadata

When we first converted our document to the EPUB format in Calibre, we indicated some basic metadata information (title, author, publisher, etc.)

To view the eBooks metadata within Sigil, select **Meta Editor...** from the **Tools** menu.

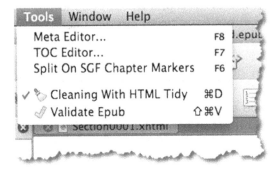

Figure 8-22: The Tools Menu

The book's current metadata will be displayed. In our example, we see the metadata we specified earlier immediately after converting the document to EPUB.

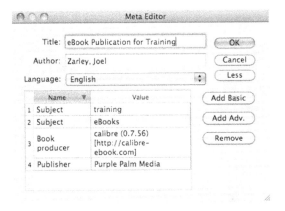

Figure 8-23: The eBook's Current Metadata

If we click the **Add Basic** button in this dialog box, we will be presented with a list of additional, commonly used metadata items.

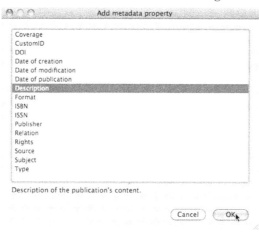

Figure 8-24: Add Basic Metadata

Selecting a metadata item (or, multi-selecting several) and clicking OK will add the selected field(s) to the metadata dialog window in *Figure 8-23*. From there, you can specify the desired values for these fields.

If the "basic" metadata does not provide appropriate options, the advanced list (**Add Adv.** button) will allow you to choose from all the currently available metadata items supported by EPUB.

Figure 8-25: Add Advanced Metadata

Working with the TOC

The table-of-contents (TOC) is very important because it allows fast and easy navigation within your book by readers. The TOC is defined by the styles you have associated to the text in a hierarchical format. For example, a style defined as "Heading 1" is the highest level of the TOC; subsequent text defined as "Heading 2" (but occurring before the next "Heading 1") would be indicated as a sub-set of the "Heading 1" information in the TOC. The TOC is automatically generated by Sigil.

To work with or view the TOC, select **TOC Editor...** from the **Tools** menu. (See *Figure 8-22* as a reference.)

Figure 8-26: The TOC Editor

To remove an item from the TOC, scroll to the far right of the editor window and deselect the checkbox in the **Include** column for that item. (Note that this column is not visible in Figure 8-26.) To add that item back into the TOC later, deselect the **TOC items only** checkbox, which will display all items indicated with a heading style (1-6) in the document. Then, just select to include the item in the TOC again.

You can also edit the text displayed in the TOC by double-clicking an entry and typing a revised title. However, this not only changes how the entry is displayed to the reader in the TOC, but also changes the text within the content to match your edits. (This occurs because the TOC entry is tied directly to the corresponding content in the document by nature of the heading style applied.)

Testing the Finished Work

After you have done all the work of formatting and publishing your eBook, you will want to test your final publication before distributing it to your students.

This can be accomplished in two processes (and both are recommended):

- Run the EPUB check utility on the file; and

- Test the book in an eReader.

EPUB Validation Check

The IDPF offers a utility to check the integrity and validation of EPUB files. The stand-alone utility is available for free download at:

http://code.google.com/p/epubcheck/

In addition, Sigil contains a built-in EPUB validation utility. The utility can be launched via the **Tools** menu and selecting **Validate Epub**. (See Figure 8-22 as a reference.)

While it is very important that your publishing process produce valid EPUB files, often items found by the validation utility do not always impact how your eBooks are viewed by students. (Many of the eReaders are actually somewhat "forgiving" in their interpretation of eBooks.)

Most retail eBookstores (Apple iBooks, Kobo, Barnes and Noble, etc.) require that your EPUB successfully pass validation to be listed in their store. However, if you are distributing your eBooks to groups of students internally this may not be a significant concern for you. Conducting a "real life" usability test of your book within an eReader may be the best testing you can do. (This is particularly true if you are able to test on each of the eReader platforms your students may be using.)

Test the Book in an eReader

The best way to check your document to ensure that it will display to students as intended is to check it directly within an eReader. (See Chapter 9 for more information.)

After you save the EPUB file it can be moved to your eReader device for testing. It can be read directly as an EPUB in iBooks, Nook, Kobo, Sony, and most other eReaders. If you wish to view it on a Kindle, you will first need to convert it to MOBI format using Calibre.

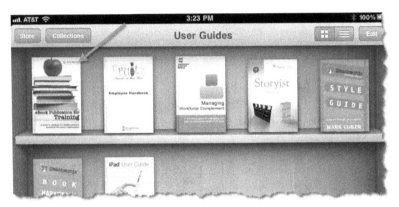

Figure 8-27: Viewing the Content in Apple iBooks

After you load the eBook into the reader you can test the content for viewing or other problems, then make note of those so that you can fix those items in Sigil. Keep in mind that different eReaders can display the exact same eBook file with variations, so if possible you should attempt to test on the devices your students will be using.

CHAPTER 9

Distributing the eBook

Now that you have converted your learning material to eBook, the only step is to get it out to your students! This chapter will cover various methods of distributing your eBooks.

Means of Distribution

There are various methods possible for getting your training material loaded onto your students' eReading devices. At a high level, these include:

- Using eBook management software;

- Manual file management; and

- Retail publication

eBook Management Software

We have mentioned a few eBook management tools earlier when talking about the conversion of files to eBook format (Calibre and Adobe Digital Editions). Apple iTunes could also be considered an eBook management system.

In each case, the applications give you the ability to store and organize the book files on a computer, while sharing them across reading devices.

Calibre

In Chapter 8 we spent quite a bit of time in the Calibre tool, using it to convert our formatted HTML file into EPUB format. And, while conversion is one of Calibre's strengths, it is also a very good eBook manager.

Calibre allows you to categorize your eBook library, and "tag" books for quick access later. When an eReader device is attached to your computer, Calibre recognizes it and activates a "send to device" function which allows you to easily copy books from your Calibre library to your eReader device.

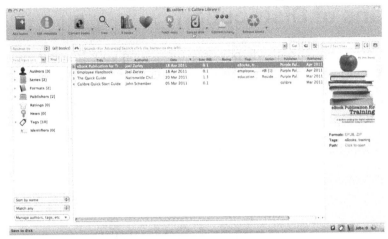

Figure 9-1: The Calibre eBook Management Tool

See Chapter 8 for information about how to download Calibre.

Adobe Digital Editions

Like Calibre, Adobe Digital Editions allows you to view and manage eBook libraries. It also provides the ability to copy eBooks in the library directly to an eReader device.

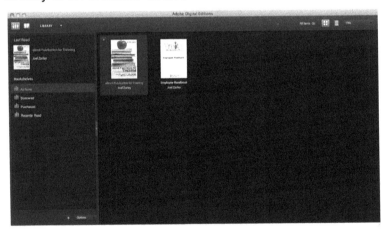

Figure 9-2: Adobe Digital Editions

Digital Editions is considered part of Adobe's overall digital publishing platform (along with the authoring/layout application InDesign). The Digital Editions standalone application is available for free download at:

http://www.adobe.com/products/digitaleditions

Apple iTunes

While iTunes is primarily thought of as a music management system, iTunes is also the vehicle that Apple uses to transfer eBooks to the iPad, iPhone, and other Apple devices.

While not as full featured of an eBook management system as Calibre or Digital Editions (iTunes is not intended to be a dedicated eBook library), it does allow you to organize by title, author, and subject.

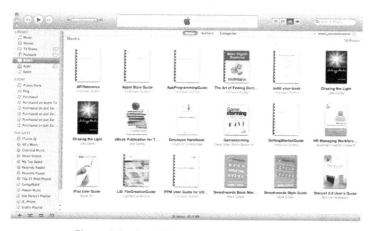

Figure 9-3: eBook Management in Apple iTunes

Like Calibre and Adobe Digital Editions, iTunes is available for free download at:

http://www.apple.com/itunes

Manual File Management

The eBook library management tools listed in the previous section provide ways to store, organize, and transfer your books. However, there are even simpler techniques which can be used to place content on an eReader.

Wired Connection

Nearly all of the eReader devices (Kindle, Nook, Sony Reader, etc.) allow you to directly connect the device to a computer, usually using a USB cable. In essence, your computer will interpret the eReader as an externally connected disk drive. You can simply move the files from your computer to the eReader, just as you would with any other attached drive.

E-Mail

Nearly all of the eReader devices (including the iPad and iPhone) allow you to e-mail eBook files then have them opened on the eBook reader. A few of the devices (like the Kindle) actually set up a separate e-mail address unique to the eReader.

Retail Publication

As the ultimate way to distribute your book, you can actually publish it and make it available for download on many eBookstore web sites. At any of these sites you have the option of offering the book for free, or charging for it.

Keep in mind that if you decide to publish your book this way that you are making your content "public" at that point. So, for most internal training documents this probably would not be an appropriate distribution method.

However, if you work for an institution that does have an opportunity for public information sharing, or are a consultant that has the ability to monetize your information and expertise, this can be an excellent means of distribution.

Amazon Kindle Store

Amazon provides individuals with the ability to publish their work directly to the Kindle store. There is an upload utility that enables processing of your formatted HTML document to the Kindle format. Publishing via Amazon is a free service.

You can get more information about publishing to the Kindle store at:

http://kdp.amazon.com

Barnes & Noble Nook Store

Just like Amazon, Barnes & Noble allows the opportunity to publish directly in their Nook eBookstore, through a free service called PubIt.

You can get more information about the PubIt service at:

http://pubit.barnesandnoble.com

Smashwords

We talked about Smashwords in Chapter 7 on the topic of formatting our training material for conversion to eBook. Smashwords also offers free eBook publishing to independent authors.

Unlike Amazon and Barnes & Noble, however, Smashwords is an aggregator of eBooks. So, they not only can distribute your eBook through their own storefront, but they also will distribute to other major eBookstores. Currently, their distribution includes:

- Apple iBooks
- Barnes & Noble
- Sony Reader Store
- Kobo
- Diesel eBooks
- Stanza
- Scrollmotion (for publication as smart phone apps)

More information about publishing on Smashwords can be found at:

http://www.smashwords.com/about/how_to_publish_on_smashwords/

CHAPTER 10
The Last Word

Summary

I hope you have found this book useful, and through the course of it you have determined uses for eBook training materials at your organization.

If you have read this far, you now have the basic information necessary to convert your existing learning content to eBook format (or, even create an eBook from scratch). Of course, like any other technical skill, the more you practice with this workflow, the more comfortable you will become.

The world of eBooks and eReaders is changing very rapidly. Even in the course of the few short months that it took me to write this book, the technology (and acceptance of that technology) has grown significantly. The resources listed in this book (like the Mobile Read Wiki) will be great resources for you to help keep up with this rapidly changing landscape.

Contact Me

Please feel free to contact with any comments or suggestions for improving future editions of this book, or to share your own experiences with publishing eBooks for learning content.

You can contact me at:

E-mail: editor@purplepalmmedia.com

Twitter: @purplepalmmedia

LinkedIn: Joel Zarley

Index

A

Adobe 3
  Digital Editions 82
  InDesign 57
  PDF 3
  Portable Document Format 3
Amazon.com 4
  Kindle 4, 20
Apple 21
  iPad 21
  iTunes 83
  iWork Suite 57
AZW format 27

B

Barnes & Noble 20
  Nook 20

C

Calibre 59, 81

E

eBook Cover 55
eBook formats 25
  AZW format 27
  EPUB 28
  Mobipocket 27
  PDF 26
  TXT (text) 25
E Ink 17
EPUB 28
  EPUB File Contents 33
  Validation Check 77

I

International Digital Publishing Forum (IDPF) 31
iPad 21

K

Kindle 4, 20
Kobo eReader 20

L

LCD 17

M

Metadata 73
Mobipocket 27

N

Nook 20

P

PDF 26
Portable Document Format 26
Project Gutenberg 4

S

Semantics 73
Sigil 65
Smartphones 21
Smashwords.com 47
  Smashwords Style Guide 47
Sony Reader 19
Stylesheets 70

T

Tablet 21
TXT (text) 25

www.ingramcontent.com/pod-product-compliance
Lightning Source LLC
Chambersburg PA
CBHW060947050326

40689CB00012B/2581